This book belongs to

....

If found, please contact at

....

....

....

Scripture quotations are from

The New King James Version®. Copyright © 1982 by Thomas Nelson, Inc. Used by permission. All rights reserved.

The Holy Bible, New International Version®, NIV®. Copyright © 1973, 1978, 1984, 2011 by Biblica, Inc.® Used by permission. All rights reserved worldwide.

The Good News Translation in Today's English Version- Second Edition Copyright © 1992 by American Bible Society. Used by Permission.

The *Holy Bible*, New Living Translation, copyright © 1996, 2004, 2007, 2013 by Tyndale House Foundation. Used by permission of Tyndale House Publishers, Inc., Carol Stream, Illinois 60188. All rights reserved.

Cover and interior design by Janelle Coury

COLOR THE BIBLE is a registered trademark of The Hawkins Children's LLC. Harvest House Publishers, Inc., is the exclusive licensee of the federally registered trademark COLOR THE BIBLE.

Michal Sparks's artwork can be found throughout the home-furnishing industry in textiles, gift items, dinnerware, and more. She is the artist for *Words of Comfort for Times of Loss* and *When Someone You Love Has Cancer*. She and her family live in New Jersey.

COLOR THE PSALMS 2017 WEEKLY PLANNER
Planner copyright © 2016 by Harvest House Publishers
Artwork copyright © by Michal Sparks
Published by Harvest House Publishers
Eugene, Oregon 97402
www.harvesthousepublishers.com

ISBN 978-0-7369-6902-4 (pbk.)

Certified Sourcing
www.sfiprogram.org
SFI-00453

Printed in the United States of America

16 17 18 19 20 21 22 23 24 /ML-JC/ 10 9 8 7 6 5 4 3 2 1

2017

JANUARY

S	M	T	W	T	F	S
1	2	3	4	5	6	7
8	9	10	11	12	13	14
15	16	17	18	19	20	21
22	23	24	25	26	27	28
29	30	31				

FEBRUARY

S	M	T	W	T	F	S
			1	2	3	4
5	6	7	8	9	10	11
12	13	14	15	16	17	18
19	20	21	22	23	24	25
26	27	28				

MARCH

S	M	T	W	T	F	S
			1	2	3	4
5	6	7	8	9	10	11
12	13	14	15	16	17	18
19	20	21	22	23	24	25
26	27	28	29	30	31	

APRIL

S	M	T	W	T	F	S
						1
2	3	4	5	6	7	8
9	10	11	12	13	14	15
16	17	18	19	20	21	22
23	24	25	26	27	28	29
30						

MAY

S	M	T	W	T	F	S
	1	2	3	4	5	6
7	8	9	10	11	12	13
14	15	16	17	18	19	20
21	22	23	24	25	26	27
28	29	30	31			

JUNE

S	M	T	W	T	F	S
				1	2	3
4	5	6	7	8	9	10
11	12	13	14	15	16	17
18	19	20	21	22	23	24
25	26	27	28	29	30	

JULY

S	M	T	W	T	F	S
						1
2	3	4	5	6	7	8
9	10	11	12	13	14	15
16	17	18	19	20	21	22
23	24	25	26	27	28	29
30	31					

AUGUST

S	M	T	W	T	F	S
		1	2	3	4	5
6	7	8	9	10	11	12
13	14	15	16	17	18	19
20	21	22	23	24	25	26
27	28	29	30	31		

SEPTEMBER

S	M	T	W	T	F	S
					1	2
3	4	5	6	7	8	9
10	11	12	13	14	15	16
17	18	19	20	21	22	23
24	25	26	27	28	29	30

OCTOBER

S	M	T	W	T	F	S
1	2	3	4	5	6	7
8	9	10	11	12	13	14
15	16	17	18	19	20	21
22	23	24	25	26	27	28
29	30	31				

NOVEMBER

S	M	T	W	T	F	S
			1	2	3	4
5	6	7	8	9	10	11
12	13	14	15	16	17	18
19	20	21	22	23	24	25
26	27	28	29	30		

DECEMBER

S	M	T	W	T	F	S
					1	2
3	4	5	6	7	8	9
10	11	12	13	14	15	16
17	18	19	20	21	22	23
24	25	26	27	28	29	30
31						

2017 Important Dates

JANUARY

FEBRUARY

MARCH

APRIL

MAY

JUNE

2017 Important Dates

JULY

....
....
....
....
....

AUGUST

....
....
....
....
....

SEPTEMBER

....
....
....
....
....

OCTOBER

....
....
....
....
....

NOVEMBER

....
....
....
....
....

DECEMBER

....
....
....
....
....

Birthdays

JANUARY

··
··
··
··
··
··

FEBRUARY

··
··
··
··
··
··

MARCH

··
··
··
··
··
··

APRIL

··
··
··
··
··
··

MAY

··
··
··
··
··
··

JUNE

··
··
··
··
··
··

Birthdays

JULY

....
....
....
....
....
....

AUGUST

....
....
....
....
....
....

SEPTEMBER

....
....
....
....
....
....

OCTOBER

....
....
....
....
....
....

NOVEMBER

....
....
....
....
....
....

DECEMBER

....
....
....
....
....
....

January

Sunday	Monday	Tuesday
1	2	3
8	9	10
15	16	17
22	23	24
29	30	31

Wednesday	Thursday	Friday	Saturday
4	5	6	7
11	12	13	14
18	19	20	21
25	26	27	28

You will show me
the path of life;
in Your presence is
fullness of joy;
at Your right hand are
pleasures
forevermore.

PSALM 16:11

December / January

MON
26

TUE
27

WED
28

THUR
29

SUN
1

FRI
30

JANUARY

S	M	T	W	T	F	S
1	2	3	4	5	6	7
8	9	10	11	12	13	14
15	16	17	18	19	20	21
22	23	24	25	26	27	28
29	30	31	1	2	3	4

A wonderful future awaits those who love peace

PSALM 37:37

January

MON
2

TUE
3

WED
4

THUR
5

FRI
6

SAT
7

SUN
8

JANUARY						
S	M	T	W	T	F	S
1	2	3	4	5	6	7
8	9	10	11	12	13	14
15	16	17	18	19	20	21
22	23	24	25	26	27	28
29	30	31	1	2	3	4

The Lord is my shepherd; I shall not want.
He makes me to lie down in green pastures;
He leads me beside the still waters.
He restores my soul.

PSALM 23:1-3

MON
9

SAT
14

TUE
10

WED
11

SUN
15

THUR
12

FRI
13

JANUARY

S	M	T	W	T	F	S
1	2	3	4	5	6	7
8	9	10	11	12	13	14
15	16	17	18	19	20	21
22	23	24	25	26	27	28
29	30	31	1	2	3	4

Your word is
a lamp to my feet
and a light to
my path.

PSALM 119:105

January

MON
16

TUE
17

WED
18

THUR
19

FRI
20

SAT
21

SUN
22

JANUARY

S	M	T	W	T	F	S
1	2	3	4	5	6	7
8	9	10	11	12	13	14
15	16	17	18	19	20	21
22	23	24	25	26	27	28
29	30	31	1	2	3	4

the LORD is my shepherd

PSALM 23:1

January

MON
23

TUE
24

WED
25

THUR
26

FRI
27

SAT
28

SUN
29

JANUARY

S	M	T	W	T	F	S
1	2	3	4	5	6	7
8	9	10	11	12	13	14
15	16	17	18	19	20	21
22	23	24	25	26	27	28
29	30	31	1	2	3	4

The salvation of
the righteous
is from the LORD;
He is their strength
in the time of trouble.

PSALM 37:39

January / February

MON
30

TUE
31

WED
1

THUR
2

FRI
3

SAT
4

SUN
5

JANUARY						
S	M	T	W	T	F	S
1	2	3	4	5	6	7
8	9	10	11	12	13	14
15	16	17	18	19	20	21
22	23	24	25	26	27	28
29	30	31	1	2	3	4

February

Sunday	Monday	Tuesday
5	6	7
12	13	14
19	20	21
26	27	28

Wednesday	Thursday	Friday	Saturday
1	2	3	4
8	9	10	11
15	16	17	18
22	23	24	25

I trust in your
unfailing love;
my heart rejoices in
your salvation.

PSALM 13:5

February

MON
6

SAT
11

TUE
7

WED
8

SUN
12

THUR
9

FRI
10

FEBRUARY

S	M	T	W	T	F	S
29	30	31	1	2	3	4
5	6	7	8	9	10	11
12	13	14	15	16	17	18
19	20	21	22	23	24	25
26	27	28	1	2	3	4

Be still and know that I am God

PSALM 46:10

February

MON
13

TUE
14

WED
15

THUR
16

FRI
17

SAT
18

SUN
19

FEBRUARY						
S	M	T	W	T	F	S
29	30	31	1	2	3	4
5	6	7	8	9	10	11
12	13	14	15	16	17	18
19	20	21	22	23	24	25
26	27	28	1	2	3	4

Restore to me the
joy of Your salvation,
and uphold me by
Your generous Spirit.

PSALM 51:12

February

MON
20

TUE
21

WED
22

THUR
23

FRI
24

SAT
25

SUN
26

FEBRUARY						
S	M	T	W	T	F	S
29	30	31	1	2	3	4
5	6	7	8	9	10	11
12	13	14	15	16	17	18
19	20	21	22	23	24	25
26	27	28	1	2	3	4

The LORD is my light and my Salvation

PSALM 27:1

MON
27

SAT
4

TUE
28

WED
1

SUN
5

THUR
2

FRI
3

FEBRUARY						
S	M	T	W	T	F	S
29	30	31	1	2	3	4
5	6	7	8	9	10	11
12	13	14	15	16	17	18
19	20	21	22	23	24	25
26	27	28	1	2	3	4

March

Sunday	Monday	Tuesday
5	6	7
12	13	14
19	20	21
26	27	28

Wednesday	Thursday	Friday	Saturday
1	2	3	4
8	9	10	11
15	16	17	18
22	23	24	25
29	30	31	

Under His wings you shall take refuge.

PSALM 91:4

March

MON

6

TUE

7

WED

8

THUR

9

FRI

10

SAT

11

SUN

12

MARCH						
S	M	T	W	T	F	S
26	27	28	1	2	3	4
5	6	7	8	9	10	11
12	13	14	15	16	17	18
19	20	21	22	23	24	25
26	27	28	29	30	31	1

Teach me to
do Your will,
for You are my God;
Your Spirit is good.

Lead me in the land
of uprightness.

PSALM 143:10

March

MON
13

TUE
14

WED
15

THUR
16

FRI
17

SAT
18

SUN
19

MARCH						
S	M	T	W	T	F	S
26	27	28	1	2	3	4
5	6	7	8	9	10	11
12	13	14	15	16	17	18
19	20	21	22	23	24	25
26	27	28	29	30	31	1

You have granted him unending blessings
and made him glad
with the joy of your presence.

PSALM 21:6

March

MON
20

TUE
21

WED
22

THUR
23

FRI
24

SAT
25

SUN
26

MARCH						
S	M	T	W	T	F	S
26	27	28	1	2	3	4
5	6	7	8	9	10	11
12	13	14	15	16	17	18
19	20	21	22	23	24	25
26	27	28	29	30	31	1

March / April

MON
27

TUE
28

WED
29

THUR
30

FRI
31

SAT
1

SUN
2

MARCH						
S	M	T	W	T	F	S
26	27	28	1	2	3	4
5	6	7	8	9	10	11
12	13	14	15	16	17	18
19	20	21	22	23	24	25
26	27	28	29	30	31	1

April

Sunday	Monday	Tuesday
2	3	4
9	10	11
16	17	18
23	24	25
30		

Wednesday	Thursday	Friday	Saturday
			1
5	6	7	8
12	13	14	15
19	20	21	22
26	27	28	29

APR

O Lord, my Strength & my redeemer

PSALM 19:14

April

MON

3

TUE

4

WED

5

THUR

6

FRI

7

SAT

8

SUN

9

APR

	APRIL					
S	M	T	W	T	F	S
26	27	28	29	30	31	1
2	3	4	5	6	7	8
9	10	11	12	13	14	15
16	17	18	19	20	21	22
23	24	25	26	27	28	29
30	1	2	3	4	5	6

I will
meditate on the
*glorious splendor of
Your majesty, and on
Your wondrous works.*

PSALM 145:5

MON
10

TUE
11

WED
12

THUR
13

FRI
14

SAT
15

SUN
16

APRIL

S	M	T	W	T	F	S
26	27	28	29	30	31	1
2	3	4	5	6	7	8
9	10	11	12	13	14	15
16	17	18	19	20	21	22
23	24	25	26	27	28	29
30	1	2	3	4	5	6

He heals the broken hearted.

PSALM 147:3

MON
17

SAT
22

TUE
18

WED
19

SUN
23

THUR
20

FRI
21

APRIL

S	M	T	W	T	F	S
26	27	28	29	30	31	1
2	3	4	5	6	7	8
9	10	11	12	13	14	15
16	17	18	19	20	21	22
23	24	25	26	27	28	29
30	1	2	3	4	5	6

All the paths of the LORD are
mercy and truth,
to such as keep His covenant
and His testimonies.

PSALM 25:10

April

MON
24

TUE
25

WED
26

THUR
27

FRI
28

SAT
29

SUN
30

			APRIL			
S	M	T	W	T	F	S
26	27	28	29	30	31	1
2	3	4	5	6	7	8
9	10	11	12	13	14	15
16	17	18	19	20	21	22
23	24	25	26	27	28	29
30	1	2	3	4	5	6

May

Sunday	Monday	Tuesday
	1	2
7	8	9
14	15	16
21	22	23
28	29	30

Wednesday	Thursday	Friday	Saturday
3	4	5	6
10	11	12	13
17	18	19	20
24	25	26	27
31			

Delight yourself
also in the Lord,
and He shall give you
the desires of your heart.

PSALM 37:4

May

MON
1

TUE
2

WED
3

THUR
4

FRI
5

SAT
6

SUN
7

MAY						
S	M	T	W	T	F	S
30	1	2	3	4	5	6
7	8	9	10	11	12	13
14	15	16	17	18	19	20
21	22	23	24	25	26	27
28	29	30	31	1	2	3

He hears my voice & my prayer for Mercy.

PSALM 116:1

MON
8

TUE
9

WED
10

THUR
11

FRI
12

SAT
13

SUN
14

			MAY			
S	M	T	W	T	F	S
30	1	2	3	4	5	6
7	8	9	10	11	12	13
14	15	16	17	18	19	20
21	22	23	24	25	26	27
28	29	30	31	1	2	3

My cup runs over.
Surely goodness and mercy shall follow me
all the days of my life;
and I will dwell in the house of the Lord forever.

Psalm 23:5-6

May

MON
15

TUE
16

WED
17

THUR
18

FRI
19

SAT
20

SUN
21

MAY

S	M	T	W	T	F	S
30	1	2	3	4	5	6
7	8	9	10	11	12	13
14	15	16	17	18	19	20
21	22	23	24	25	26	27
28	29	30	31	1	2	3

How precious
are your thoughts
about me, O God.

They cannot be numbered!

PSALM 139:17

May

MON
22

TUE
23

WED
24

THUR
25

FRI
26

SAT
27

SUN
28

MAY						
S	M	T	W	T	F	S
30	1	2	3	4	5	6
7	8	9	10	11	12	13
14	15	16	17	18	19	20
21	22	23	24	25	26	27
28	29	30	31	1	2	3

The Lord has done great things for us.

PSALM 126:3

May/June

MON
29

TUE
30

WED
31

THUR
1

FRI
2

SAT
3

SUN
4

MAY

JUN

MAY						
S	M	T	W	T	F	S
30	1	2	3	4	5	6
7	8	9	10	11	12	13
14	15	16	17	18	19	20
21	22	23	24	25	26	27
28	29	30	31	1	2	3

June

Sunday	Monday	Tuesday
4	5	6
11	12	13
18	19	20
25	26	27

Wednesday	Thursday	Friday	Saturday
	1	2	3
7	8	9	10
14	15	16	17
21	22	23	24
28	29	30	

JUN

Cast your burden
on the Lord,
and He shall sustain you;
He shall never permit
the righteous to be moved.

Psalm 55:22

June

MON
5

TUE
6

WED
7

THUR
8

FRI
9

SAT
10

SUN
11

		JUNE			
S	M	T	W	T	F	S
28	29	30	31	1	2	3
4	5	6	7	8	9	10
11	12	13	14	15	16	17
18	19	20	21	22	23	24
25	26	27	28	29	30	1

The Lord is near to ALL who Call on Him

PSALM 145:18

June

MON
12

TUE
13

WED
14

THUR
15

FRI
16

SAT
17

SUN
18

			JUNE			
S	M	T	W	T	F	S
28	29	30	31	1	2	3
4	5	6	7	8	9	10
11	12	13	14	15	16	17
18	19	20	21	22	23	24
25	26	27	28	29	30	1

This is the day
the Lord has made;
we will rejoice and
be glad in it.

PSALM 118:24

June

MON
19

TUE
20

WED
21

THUR
22

FRI
23

SAT
24

SUN
25

			JUNE			
S	M	T	W	T	F	S
28	29	30	31	1	2	3
4	5	6	7	8	9	10
11	12	13	14	15	16	17
18	19	20	21	22	23	24
25	26	27	28	29	30	1

God is our refuge and strength,
a very present help in trouble.

Psalm 46:1

MON
26

SAT
1

TUE
27

WED
28

SUN
2

JUN

JUL

THUR
29

FRI
30

JUNE						
S	M	T	W	T	F	S
28	29	30	31	1	2	3
4	5	6	7	8	9	10
11	12	13	14	15	16	17
18	19	20	21	22	23	24
25	26	27	28	29	30	1

July

Sunday	Monday	Tuesday
2	3	4
9	10	11
16	17	18
23	24	25
30	31	

Wednesday	Thursday	Friday	Saturday
			1
5	6	7	8
12	13	14	15
19	20	21	22
26	27	28	29

JUL

He alone is my rock and my salvation.

PSALM 62:2

July

MON
3

TUE
4

WED
5

THUR
6

FRI
7

SAT
8

SUN
9

JULY

S	M	T	W	T	F	S
25	26	27	28	29	30	1
2	3	4	5	6	7	8
9	10	11	12	13	14	15
16	17	18	19	20	21	22
23	24	25	26	27	28	29
30	31	1	2	3	4	5

Show me Your ways, O LORD;
teach me Your paths.
*Lead me in Your truth
and teach me.*

PSALM 25:4-5

July

MON
10

TUE
11

WED
12

THUR
13

FRI
14

SAT
15

SUN
16

			JULY			
S	M	T	W	T	F	S
25	26	27	28	29	30	1
2	3	4	5	6	7	8
9	10	11	12	13	14	15
16	17	18	19	20	21	22
23	24	25	26	27	28	29
30	31	1	2	3	4	5

I will praise You,
for I am *fearfully* and
wonderfully made;
marvelous are Your works,
and that my soul
knows very well.

PSALM 139:14

July

MON
17

TUE
18

WED
19

THUR
20

FRI
21

SAT
22

SUN
23

JULY						
S	M	T	W	T	F	S
25	26	27	28	29	30	1
2	3	4	5	6	7	8
9	10	11	12	13	14	15
16	17	18	19	20	21	22
23	24	25	26	27	28	29
30	31	1	2	3	4	5

Create a pure ♥ in me O GOD

PSALM 51:10

July

MON
24

TUE
25

WED
26

THUR
27

FRI
28

SAT
29

SUN
30

JUL

JULY

S	M	T	W	T	F	S
25	26	27	28	29	30	1
2	3	4	5	6	7	8
9	10	11	12	13	14	15
16	17	18	19	20	21	22
23	24	25	26	27	28	29
30	31	1	2	3	4	5

Let the morning
bring me word of
your unfailing love.

Psalm 143:8

July / August

MON
31

TUE
1

WED
2

THUR
3

FRI
4

SAT
5

SUN
6

JUL

AUG

JULY

S	M	T	W	T	F	S
25	26	27	28	29	30	1
2	3	4	5	6	7	8
9	10	11	12	13	14	15
16	17	18	19	20	21	22
23	24	25	26	27	28	29
30	31	1	2	3	4	5

August

		1
6	7	8
13	14	15
20	21	22
27	28	29

Wednesday	Thursday	Friday	Saturday
2	3	4	5
9	10	11	12
16	17	18	19
23	24	25	26
30	31		

AUG

GOD is the strength of my & my portion forever.

PSALM 73:26

August

MON
7

TUE
8

WED
9

THUR
10

FRI
11

SAT
12

SUN
13

AUG

| AUGUST | | | | | | |
S	M	T	W	T	F	S
30	31	1	2	3	4	5
6	7	8	9	10	11	12
13	14	15	16	17	18	19
20	21	22	23	24	25	26
27	28	29	30	31	1	2

Praise the Lord,
who carries our burdens
day after day;
he is the God
who saves us.

PSALM 68:19

August

MON
14

TUE
15

WED
16

THUR
17

FRI
18

SAT
19

SUN
20

AUGUST						
S	M	T	W	T	F	S
30	31	1	2	3	4	5
6	7	8	9	10	11	12
13	14	15	16	17	18	19
20	21	22	23	24	25	26
27	28	29	30	31	1	2

When I lie down, I go to sleep in peace;
you alone, O LORD, keep me perfectly safe.

PSALM 4:8

August

MON
21

TUE
22

WED
23

THUR
24

FRI
25

SAT
26

SUN
27

AUGUST						
S	M	T	W	T	F	S
30	31	1	2	3	4	5
6	7	8	9	10	11	12
13	14	15	16	17	18	19
20	21	22	23	24	25	26
27	28	29	30	31	1	2

He is our help and our shield.

PSALM 33:20

August / September

MON
28

TUE
29

WED
30

THUR
31

FRI
1

SAT
2

SUN
3

AUG

SEP

AUGUST

S	M	T	W	T	F	S
30	31	1	2	3	4	5
6	7	8	9	10	11	12
13	14	15	16	17	18	19
20	21	22	23	24	25	26
27	28	29	30	31	1	2

September

Sunday	Monday	Tuesday
3	4	5
10	11	12
17	18	19
24	25	26

Wednesday	Thursday	Friday	Saturday
		1	2
6	7	8	9
13	14	15	16
20	21	22	23
27	28	29	30

SEP

Yea, though I walk
through the valley of
the shadow of death,
I will fear no evil;
for You are with me;
Your rod and Your staff,
they comfort me.

PSALM 23:4

September

MON
4

TUE
5

WED
6

THUR
7

FRI
8

SAT
9

SUN
10

SEP

SEPTEMBER						
S	M	T	W	T	F	S
27	28	29	30	31	1	2
3	4	5	6	7	8	9
10	11	12	13	14	15	16
17	18	19	20	21	22	23
24	25	26	27	28	29	30

When my heart is overwhelmed;
lead me to the rock that is higher than I.

PSALM 61:2

September

MON 11	**SAT** 16
TUE 12	
WED 13	**SUN** 17
THUR 14	
FRI 15	

SEPTEMBER

S	M	T	W	T	F	S
27	28	29	30	31	1	2
3	4	5	6	7	8	9
10	11	12	13	14	15	16
17	18	19	20	21	22	23
24	25	26	27	28	29	30

The LORD gives
strength to his people
and
blesses them with peace.

PSALM 29.11

September

MON
18

TUE
19

WED
20

THUR
21

FRI
22

SAT
23

SUN
24

SEPTEMBER

S	M	T	W	T	F	S
27	28	29	30	31	1	2
3	4	5	6	7	8	9
10	11	12	13	14	15	16
17	18	19	20	21	22	23
24	25	26	27	28	29	30

I lift up my eyes to the hills... my help comes from the Lord.

PSALM 121:1-2

September/October

MON
25

SAT
30

TUE
26

WED
27

SUN
1

THUR
28

FRI
29

SEP

OCT

SEPTEMBER						
S	M	T	W	T	F	S
27	28	29	30	31	1	2
3	4	5	6	7	8	9
10	11	12	13	14	15	16
17	18	19	20	21	22	23
24	25	26	27	28	29	30

October

Sunday	Monday	Tuesday
1	2	3
8	9	10
15	16	17
22	23	24
29	30	31

Wednesday	Thursday	Friday	Saturday
4	5	6	7
11	12	13	14
18	19	20	21
25	26	27	28

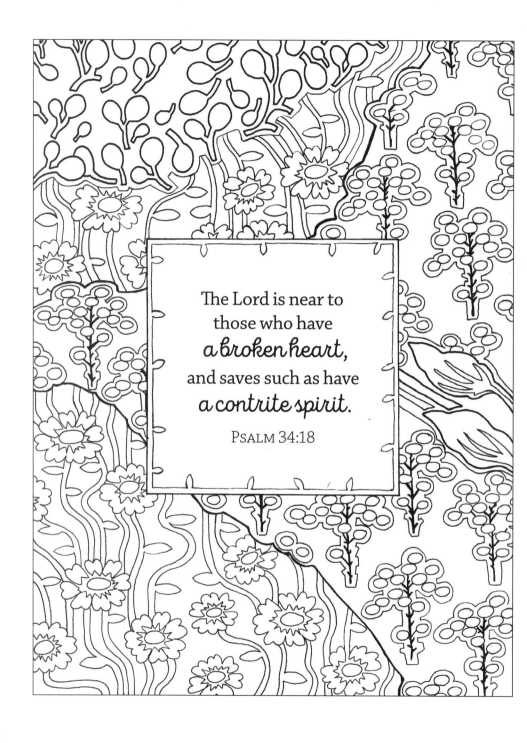

The Lord is near to
those who have
a broken heart,
and saves such as have
a contrite spirit.

PSALM 34:18

October

MON
2

TUE
3

WED
4

THUR
5

FRI
6

SAT
7

SUN
8

OCT

OCTOBER

S	M	T	W	T	F	S
1	2	3	4	5	6	7
8	9	10	11	12	13	14
15	16	17	18	19	20	21
22	23	24	25	26	27	28
29	30	31	1	2	3	4

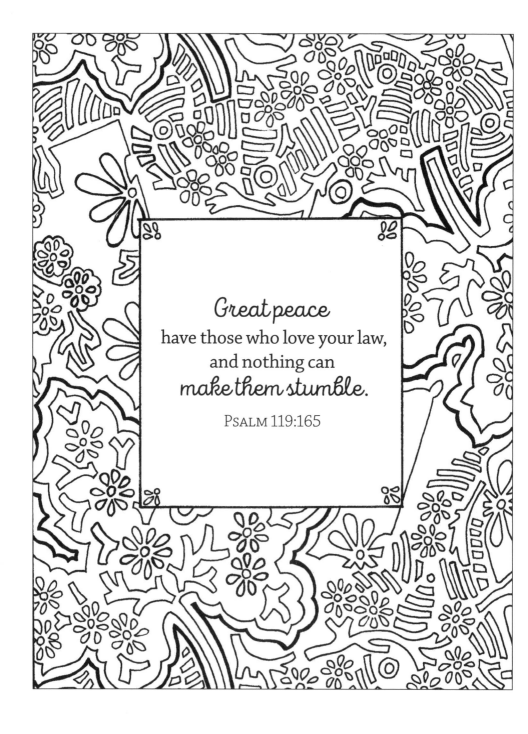

Great peace
have those who love your law,
and nothing can
make them stumble.

PSALM 119:165

October

MON
9

TUE
10

WED
11

THUR
12

FRI
13

SAT
14

SUN
15

OCT

OCTOBER

S	M	T	W	T	F	S
1	2	3	4	5	6	7
8	9	10	11	12	13	14
15	16	17	18	19	20	21
22	23	24	25	26	27	28
29	30	31	1	2	3	4

The earth is the Lord's,
and all its fullness,
the world and those who dwell therein.

Psalm 24:1

MON
16

TUE
17

WED
18

THUR
19

FRI
20

SAT
21

SUN
22

OCTOBER						
S	M	T	W	T	F	S
1	2	3	4	5	6	7
8	9	10	11	12	13	14
15	16	17	18	19	20	21
22	23	24	25	26	27	28
29	30	31	1	2	3	4

Give thanks to the Lord,
for He is good!
For His mercy endures
forever.

PSALM 107:1

October

MON
23

TUE
24

WED
25

THUR
26

FRI
27

SAT
28

SUN
29

OCTOBER

S	M	T	W	T	F	S
1	2	3	4	5	6	7
8	9	10	11	12	13	14
15	16	17	18	19	20	21
22	23	24	25	26	27	28
29	30	31	1	2	3	4

For the Lord God
is a sun and shield;
the Lord will
give grace and glory.

PSALM 84:11

MON
30

TUE
31

WED
1

THUR
2

FRI
3

SAT
4

SUN
5

OCTOBER						
S	M	T	W	T	F	S
1	2	3	4	5	6	7
8	9	10	11	12	13	14
15	16	17	18	19	20	21
22	23	24	25	26	27	28
29	30	31	1	2	3	4

OCT

NOV

November

Sunday	Monday	Tuesday
5	6	7
12	13	14
19	20	21
26	27	28

Wednesday	Thursday	Friday	Saturday
1	2	3	4
8	9	10	11
15	16	17	18
22	23	24	25
29	30		

I sought the Lord, and

He heard me,

and delivered me
from all my fears.

PSALM 34:4

November

MON
6

TUE
7

WED
8

THUR
9

FRI
10

SAT
11

SUN
12

NOVEMBER

S	M	T	W	T	F	S
29	30	31	1	2	3	4
5	6	7	8	9	10	11
12	13	14	15	16	17	18
19	20	21	22	23	24	25
26	27	28	29	30	1	2

Trust in the LORD and do good.

PSALM 37:3

November

MON
13

TUE
14

WED
15

THUR
16

FRI
17

SAT
18

SUN
19

NOVEMBER

S	M	T	W	T	F	S
29	30	31	1	2	3	4
5	6	7	8	9	10	11
12	13	14	15	16	17	18
19	20	21	22	23	24	25
26	27	28	29	30	1	2

Our help is in the name of the Lord,
who made heaven and earth.

PSALM 124:8

November

MON
20

TUE
21

WED
22

THUR
23

FRI
24

SAT
25

SUN
26

NOVEMBER

S	M	T	W	T	F	S
29	30	31	1	2	3	4
5	6	7	8	9	10	11
12	13	14	15	16	17	18
19	20	21	22	23	24	25
26	27	28	29	30	1	2

In your
unfailing love,
O God,
answer my prayer
with your
sure salvation.

PSALM 69:13

November/December

MON
27

TUE
28

WED
29

THUR
30

FRI
1

SAT
2

SUN
3

NOVEMBER						
S	M	T	W	T	F	S
29	30	31	1	2	3	4
5	6	7	8	9	10	11
12	13	14	15	16	17	18
19	20	21	22	23	24	25
26	27	28	29	30	1	2

NOV

DEC

December

Sunday	Monday	Tuesday
3	4	5
10	11	12
17	18	19
24	25	26
31		

Wednesday	Thursday	Friday	Saturday
		1	2
6	7	8	9
13	14	15	16
20	21	22	23
27	28	29	30

DEC

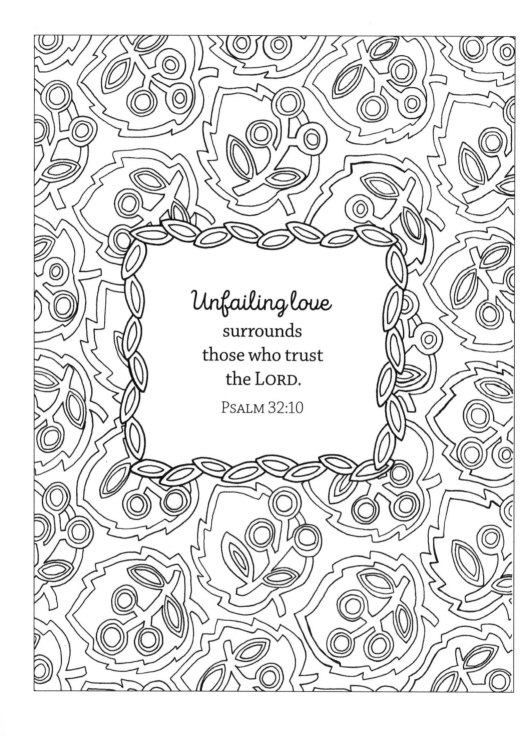

Unfailing love
surrounds
those who trust
the LORD.

PSALM 32:10

December

MON
4

TUE
5

WED
6

THUR
7

FRI
8

SAT
9

SUN
10

DECEMBER						
S	M	T	W	T	F	S
26	27	28	29	30	1	2
3	4	5	6	7	8	9
10	11	12	13	14	15	16
17	18	19	20	21	22	23
24	25	26	27	28	29	30
31	1	2	3	4	5	6

DEC

PSALM 33:20

December

MON
11

TUE
12

WED
13

THUR
14

FRI
15

SAT
16

SUN
17

DECEMBER

S	M	T	W	T	F	S
26	27	28	29	30	1	2
3	4	5	6	7	8	9
10	11	12	13	14	15	16
17	18	19	20	21	22	23
24	25	26	27	28	29	30
31	1	2	3	4	5	6

DEC

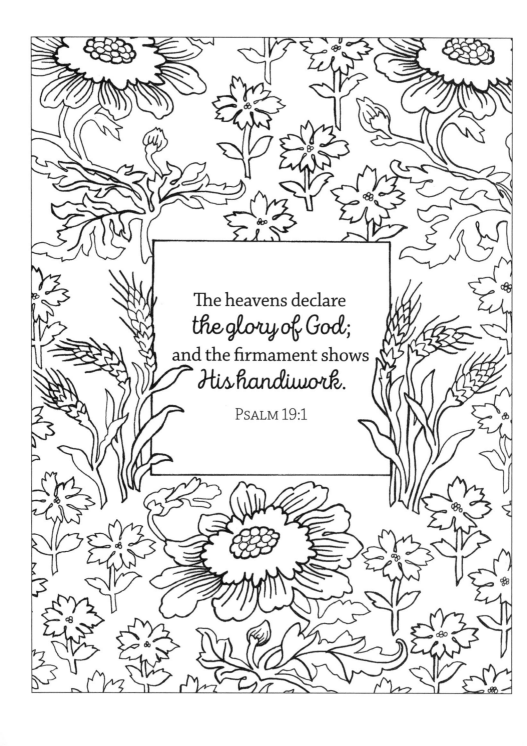

The heavens declare
the glory of God;
and the firmament shows
His handiwork.

PSALM 19:1

December

MON
18

TUE
19

WED
20

THUR
21

FRI
22

SAT
23

SUN
24

DECEMBER						
S	M	T	W	T	F	S
26	27	28	29	30	1	2
3	4	5	6	7	8	9
10	11	12	13	14	15	16
17	18	19	20	21	22	23
24	25	26	27	28	29	30
31	1	2	3	4	5	6

You make your saving help my shield,
and your right hand sustains me.

PSALM 18:35

December

MON
25

TUE
26

WED
27

THUR
28

FRI
29

SAT
30

SUN
31

DECEMBER						
S	M	T	W	T	F	S
26	27	28	29	30	1	2
3	4	5	6	7	8	9
10	11	12	13	14	15	16
17	18	19	20	21	22	23
24	25	26	27	28	29	30
31	1	2	3	4	5	6

DEC

2018 Important Dates

JANUARY

··
··
··
··
··
··

FEBRUARY

··
··
··
··
··
··

MARCH

··
··
··
··
··

APRIL

··
··
··
··
··

MAY

··
··
··
··
··
··

JUNE

··
··
··
··
··
··

2018 Important Dates

JULY

....
....
....
....
....
....

AUGUST

....
....
....
....
....
....

SEPTEMBER

....
....
....
....
....
....

OCTOBER

....
....
....
....
....
....

NOVEMBER

....
....
....
....
....
....

DECEMBER

....
....
....
....
....
....

Addresses

NAME:

ADDRESS:

CITY: STATE: ZIP CODE:

PHONE #: EMAIL:

NAME:

ADDRESS:

CITY: STATE: ZIP CODE:

PHONE #: EMAIL:

NAME:

ADDRESS:

CITY: STATE: ZIP CODE:

PHONE #: EMAIL:

NAME:

ADDRESS:

CITY: STATE: ZIP CODE:

PHONE #: EMAIL:

NAME:

ADDRESS:

CITY: STATE: ZIP CODE:

PHONE #: EMAIL:

Addresses

NAME:
ADDRESS:
CITY: STATE: ZIP CODE:
PHONE #:   EMAIL:

NAME:
ADDRESS:
CITY: STATE: ZIP CODE:
PHONE #:   EMAIL:

NAME:
ADDRESS:
CITY: STATE: ZIP CODE:
PHONE #:   EMAIL:

NAME:
ADDRESS:
CITY: STATE: ZIP CODE:
PHONE #:   EMAIL:

NAME:
ADDRESS:
CITY: STATE: ZIP CODE:
PHONE #:   EMAIL:

Addresses

NAME:

ADDRESS:

CITY: STATE: ZIP CODE:

PHONE #:   EMAIL:

NAME:

ADDRESS:

CITY: STATE: ZIP CODE:

PHONE #:   EMAIL:

NAME:

ADDRESS:

CITY: STATE: ZIP CODE:

PHONE #:   EMAIL:

NAME:

ADDRESS:

CITY: STATE: ZIP CODE:

PHONE #:   EMAIL:

NAME:

ADDRESS:

CITY: STATE: ZIP CODE:

PHONE #:   EMAIL:

Addresses

NAME:

ADDRESS:

CITY: STATE: ZIP CODE:

PHONE #: EMAIL:

NAME:

ADDRESS:

CITY: STATE: ZIP CODE:

PHONE #: EMAIL:

NAME:

ADDRESS:

CITY: STATE: ZIP CODE:

PHONE #: EMAIL:

NAME:

ADDRESS:

CITY: STATE: ZIP CODE:

PHONE #: EMAIL:

NAME:

ADDRESS:

CITY: STATE: ZIP CODE:

PHONE #: EMAIL:

Passwords

WEBSITE:

USERNAME:

PASSWORD:

WEBSITE:

USERNAME:

PASSWORD:

WEBSITE:

USERNAME:

PASSWORD:

WEBSITE:

USERNAME:

PASSWORD:

WEBSITE:

USERNAME:

PASSWORD:

WEBSITE:

USERNAME:

PASSWORD:

Passwords

WEBSITE:

USERNAME:

PASSWORD:

WEBSITE:

USERNAME:

PASSWORD:

WEBSITE:

USERNAME:

PASSWORD:

WEBSITE:

USERNAME:

PASSWORD:

WEBSITE:

USERNAME:

PASSWORD:

WEBSITE:

USERNAME:

PASSWORD:

To-Do

To-Do

- ○ ....
- ○ ....
- ○ ....
- ○ ....
- ○ ....
- ○ ....
- ○ ....
- ○ ....
- ○ ....
- ○ ....
- ○ ....
- ○ ....
- ○ ....
- ○ ....
- ○ ....
- ○ ....
- ○ ....
- ○ ....
- ○ ....
- ○ ....

- ○ ....
- ○ ....
- ○ ....
- ○ ....
- ○ ....
- ○ ....
- ○ ....
- ○ ....
- ○ ....
- ○ ....
- ○ ....
- ○ ....
- ○ ....
- ○ ....
- ○ ....
- ○ ....
- ○ ....
- ○ ....
- ○ ....
- ○ ....

To-Do

To-Do

- [ ] ....
- [ ] ....
- [ ] ....
- [ ] ....
- [ ] ....
- [ ] ....
- [ ] ....
- [ ] ....
- [ ] ....
- [ ] ....
- [ ] ....
- [ ] ....
- [ ] ....
- [ ] ....
- [ ] ....
- [ ] ....
- [ ] ....
- [ ] ....
- [ ] ....
- [ ] ....

- [ ] ....
- [ ] ....
- [ ] ....
- [ ] ....
- [ ] ....
- [ ] ....
- [ ] ....
- [ ] ....
- [ ] ....
- [ ] ....
- [ ] ....
- [ ] ....
- [ ] ....
- [ ] ....
- [ ] ....
- [ ] ....
- [ ] ....
- [ ] ....
- [ ] ....
- [ ] ....

To-Do

To-Do

- ◯ ....
- ◯ ....
- ◯ ....
- ◯ ....
- ◯ ....
- ◯ ....
- ◯ ....
- ◯ ....
- ◯ ....
- ◯ ....
- ◯ ....
- ◯ ....
- ◯ ....
- ◯ ....
- ◯ ....
- ◯ ....
- ◯ ....
- ◯ ....
- ◯ ....
- ◯ ....

- ◯ ....
- ◯ ....
- ◯ ....
- ◯ ....
- ◯ ....
- ◯ ....
- ◯ ....
- ◯ ....
- ◯ ....
- ◯ ....
- ◯ ....
- ◯ ....
- ◯ ....
- ◯ ....
- ◯ ....
- ◯ ....
- ◯ ....
- ◯ ....
- ◯ ....
- ◯ ....

Notes

Notes

Notes

Notes

Notes

Notes

Notes

Notes

Notes

Notes

Notes

Notes

Notes

Notes